The *Vital* Function of Constant Narrative

*Our universe began
with the end of another.*

marlys west

V Press LC
www.vpresslc.com

Consistently committed to publishing writing that rises above.

ISBN 978-1-7330488-7-3

PRINTED IN U.S.A.

All rights reserved, including the right of reproduction in part or in whole in any form whatsoever.

The Vital Function of Constant Narrative
© 2022 by Marlys West

Praise for
The Vital Function of Constant Narrative

Whatever flows from you, you are: black bird, old dog, white cat.
This new cup.

"This line from the opening poem in Marlys West's *The Vital Function of Constant Narrative* suggests elegantly the main thread that runs throughout the collection: here is no barrier between past, present, and future; this and other worldly; the living and the dead. All that has ever been or ever will be—plant, mineral, or animal—are vital parts of the ongoing narrative of both the conscious and the unconscious. West's award winning book is a stunning collection of lyrical, wise, and haunting reminders of the connected, sacred nature of all things."

—Cathy Smith Bowers, Guest Editor and
Former Poet Laureate of North Carolina

Also by Marlys West

Evangeline was a Beauty Queen

Notes for a Late-Blooming Martyr

For Vivian, Sylvie, Owen & Phil
and for all my parents
and all my siblings
and their kids
and cats
and physics
the aunts and uncles
all the other cousins
IG friends
my Los Angeles/Montana friends
Ronni, Cora & Shannon

with love and gratitude to the artists/writers
Jenny Fleming
Ginny Wiehardt
Julie Borsa

kindest thanks to the wonderful book designer
Jessica Bell

kindest thanks to my good and lovely editor and publisher
Torie Amarie Dale

and finally with gratitude for the time and space:
Ucross Foundation
Cuttyhunk Writers Residency
Big Art Labs Los Angeles

Table of Contents

Who Came Before 13
Gallop 14
The Spin of the Chores in a Secret Pocket 16
By That I Do Mean Horse 18
Water and Color 22
Song of the Limpet 25
The Stuck Clock 27
Black Mission Fig 29
BANG 31
Ever After 33
I Eat What the Goat Eats 35
Second and Grand 36
The Knack of Dowsing 38
A History of Tranquilizers 40
The Oddest Sea 42
Forsooth 44
Everything Twice 46
If the River Sounds 48
A Collision of Satellites 51
Still Life Quail Leg on White Plate 53
Duck Egg as Low Poison 55
A Brief Collection of Villainous Faults 57
You Won't Be Needing This 59
Cowed 61
Marry the Donkey 64
Flowers Keep their Original Yellow 66
The Vital Function of Constant Narrative 68
We Made You Out of Wax 70
SMASH 72
When the Coward Goes Out 74
A Study in Accidents and Disrepair 77
Encyclopedia of the Dead 78
Unbecoming 80
Spun 81
When the President is Black 83
He Must Have Hung Us Up to Dry 85
How Many Moths Make the Weight of the Moon? 87
Signs of Imminent Breath 89
Ganzfeld Los Angeles 90
Regret and Other Bodies 92
Courage 95
Acknowledgements 97

The Vital Function of Constant Narrative

Who Came Before

Now that you are dead our trajectories diverge—with luck I might breathe in one or two carbon molecules, uncaught burnt salt from your eight big bones: *femur, tibia, fibula.*

Let me pluck you out of nature. Maybe in the forest at night when a barn owl swallows a mouse whose foot was the back of your throat. What made her tail tip? *Your humerus. Your ulna.*

Whatever flows from you, you are: black bird, old dog, white cat. This new cup. A worm. Fish fins. Moth wing. Dull eggs like chalk in a nest in a tree. *Radius.* Your wrist a black widow behind the baking tins.

The dinner could be you. The plate. It's wet. Dead I seem to love you better. Marriage was two minutes of blue fire then dying flame. What isn't? Fast forward to the midnight bedside where

I put flower water in your cup. You saw me do it. Brown algae lining a glass full of old flowers and ferns. How to put you back in feather? Your lips two leaves beneath a wren.

Your mesentery new pellets of fur and bones and bloody broken things; all that made the creature without its motions or essential features. Mouse-like but not mouse. Come

curl in my hand if you can—be the black flower's bottom of green fruit. I will press you into the ground. When will I lean against the trunk of you? All parts of you? *The seventh rib, eighth.* That I found.

Marlys West

Gallop

Like a bird's wing the hindquarters of a horse seen from the side, beautiful black paddles pushing the body through the grass of a paddock,

grass stiff as boar's whiskers but flatter. Each horse leg pumping fast and faster like the whir of factory packaging, clatter and clatter, the natural

world and its parallel automata. Manual typewriter running along clickity-clack, white paper struck repeatedly with tiny aluminum lettered bats like

the few frozen leaves on the trees in Wyoming in November. All day the deer with their mouths to the ground then back up, ears up, waiting for

danger. Last night on the ride back to the ranch our head-lights lit up a car-length of blood washed over the silver road.
Last week I found

a dead bird stiff in the snow on the windowsill—carried it in my glove and made a nest in a cottonwood tree where it
is still dead. At night

I sleep under feathers—a thousand ducks plucked for my comfort, I wear a black down coat during the day in order to keep
warm. On my walk

today I checked the deer carcass from three days ago—one leg left. Two black and white birds, their dinner interrupted, scolded
loudly. Past the dead

The Vital Function of Constant Narrative

deer by the field of dark and rust-colored bulls, I stood watching until
the nearest bull made a sound vaguely pneumatic. On the way home
I found

what looked like a dog house from fifty years ago, but when I peeked in I
saw water at the bottom, perfectly still—
an old well which made me feel

buoyed up again. I ran along snowmelt by the side of the road,
wings at my back as if I were a bird and
did not count my feathers.

Marlys West

The Spin of the Chores in a Secret Pocket

Every morning the body to be washed and food for bodies to be prepared, a plate before the clean body, body properly rinsed in water running out of some aquifer rushing over the shoulders and neck of the body in its shower. Now the coffee with its sharp smell like burnt soil and the smoky egg smell like insides cooking, wafting through the house with a layer of dust in every corner, clothes letting go their infinitesimal threads every day like the skin of the body sloughing off every hour, falling like snow into the tiles.

If we were to disappear the dogs could still find us. In the kitchen. By the front door. Along the sidewalk, along the cars.

When my oldest was a little girl another girl her age disappeared and back then I followed the case more or less closely in the way you do a famous woman pregnant the same time not a serious obsession but something to while away the time until babies come and sweep you along in their river of sleep and milk and yellow diapers, tiny umbilical stumps that tell you they have come from somewhere else, from inside you, like coming from the sun, bright and miraculous but also making perfect sense in a medical textbook way.

There you were big with fetal material, pulling the unformed creature along, letting it bounce in the bone bowl of the pelvis. When the old nurse took the babies from their plastic cribs and rinsed them you could see in the way she held their tiny necks she knew what she was doing. Not one slipped. Not one was lost to the whoopsie-daisy. Every body she counted and counted twice, same for every slippery limb. Every ankle with a collar connected to an electric alarm.

The Vital Function of Constant Narrative

This way to comfort and warm water. This way to your mother's new shoulder or your father's hands, all of your body enveloped in paper, in cotton and the food like sugar; the sugar made out of that black bloody room post small fruit, little cake for which I was waiting and the baby waiting, too for the task of the body, whatever it is, to be finished.

Marlys West

By That I Do Mean Horse

Dawdling through the mall with our mother's money,
>   father's absence ringing in our ears,
>   we were primed right out of being
>   thankful for mere existence when
>   an old friend bought brown heroin.
>   *Why?* We asked her. *Why? Why?*
>   Nothing happened. They got high.
>   Mushrooms were painful as period
>   cramps and distorted my face in the
>   mirror. Ecstasy was more realistic
>   somehow, but I never even tried it.

My old beau knew a boy who went mad smoking jimson weed,
>   screaming and writhing on cold tile
>   this friend, but alive. Two hundred
>   untreated Morning Glory seeds could
>   send all of us into the green heavens
>   of believing, but they are all *treated*.
>   See package details: *vasoconstrictor!*

Cold hands indicate affection. Cold hands indicate a problem
>   with circulation. Back then I had no
>   friends, really. Under the coke-rush,
>   just past the bag of crumble horse,
>   everyone I knew looked a bit sad.
>   *Blow! Crack!* Too wired for such
>   potent restorative, parties where I
>   got to pick, I picked hallucinogens
>   even though in the eighties there

The Vital Function of Constant Narrative

    wasn't time for some long-ass trip.
    This was the nineties and everyone
    ran to get their light parts inked in.
    Everybody at some point worked
    in a bar. One night I tossed a tray
    of empty beer bottles out a window
    because truly I'd had about enough

only really what troubles did I have?
    Who was I to be through? High or
    not you had to do it. *A one and a two...*
when they played a certain set of songs we had to hop up on the tables
    and dance along. No one asked me
    to be the shot girl at endless o'clock.
    Honestly? I didn't want it; why bark
    when you can get any dog to do it?
    It was the era of the CEO. A decade
    of blow, drinks with names like *Sex*
    on the Beach, Lady Bellini of Peach.
Once as a hippie I grew cotton just to see. Headline: It's a tree.
    The bolls are stuck on little thorns.
    I'm from the South and wanted to
    know. I was born in the city of New
    never mind. Look it up and then go.
    The okra was also unpleasant; sharp.
When it got too hot I let the whole mess turn to dust. *Adieu*, Texas.

I worked a little square by the chickens and had a dog, too, didn't I?
    I was so organic.
    Spare my earth.
    Overly pedantic.
    Now I'd old and already half plastic.

To hell with Baltimore, also. Our young landlord off skiing forgot
    to fill the basement furnace with oil.
    He laughed when he came back, said
    the snow in Austria was eiderdown;
    but snow in Baltimore will freeze your
    ask him why he gave our whole brown
    stone the shaft. What a powdery idiot.
    You know I'm talking about cocaine.

Once I let a man spend the night who talked nonstop about recovery;
    I wanted him to shut up and walk home
    but there was a blizzard raging outside.

    Fifteen more minutes of his glory
    days, I made him go, I was good
    that way in those days; unkind.

    Glad I got so good-natured before
    I died. These days I just hold the
    baby and her loose valve and cry.

A girl steals her mother's beauty so they say; all my children are perfect.
    At birth the big girl got wedged
    in the bones of the birth canal.

They used a vacuum cap to pull her out, slightly abrading her scalp.
    Nothing scarring but still, having spent nine months
    both perfect and intact, she was wounded, bleeding.
I felt we let her down. All of us. Even you reading this here
    and now, did nothing to help her.
    Howl, she said to us. And how.

The Vital Function of Constant Narrative

Every hour they stuck her heel for the blood draw; the last time
    her little foot was uncovered she knew what was coming
    and screamed. *We have to milk the heel for blood.*
We said
    it's okay.
The first lie. When we finally took her home
    Here is your bedroom! That I decorated!
    (That seems stupid now.)
she stayed in the car seat, tight fists at her sides, doing nothing,
hair dull and eyes distant and puffy as if she'd been living hard
the last few days and she had.
    I lost her father, too, and by that I don't
    mean that he died. We tried. That's all
    I can really tell you right now: we tried.
See my bridle?
See my plough?
    A little of what you fancy does you good, but I spent
    forty years
    telling lies. Forty years just getting by. Forty years
    doing just enough so the edge of my longing softened
    but never actualized.
A good beginning makes
a good ending
but the middle is always a mess inside.

Does it not have any place to go, that anguish?

Marlys West

Water and Color

The dark green. What the body wants the mouth waits for, doesn't it?

Lift this kettle, witch. Make the tea for the twiggy daughter who knows her beauty but still cannot—nor can I.

Why am I wheezing when my house still stands intact and the fires are far, far north?

A little ash never hurt anyone as far as I can tell. I said a little. Actual smoke will blacken your lungs,

stick your ribs together, push your blood like a beacon to your cadmium shoes. How do you pull pale-green

to your fingers? Make it bloom? Desolate, are you? Blue-yellow are we?

The reason I take a deep breath is because I'm sad and forget to lift my chest enough to suck air into the lungs.

By making a hollow. A vacuum. Thank you, diaphragm. *And action.*

My eyes are tired—my glasses are made of wood pulp and wet cotton for all the good they're doing.

The Vital Function of Constant Narrative

The better pair I lost, the stronger. False meaning is under-
rated. The kidneys work hard for the good of your body

but when to them dost thou pray? Pray never?
The liver waxes and wanes in the body, full of blood at night

less in the morning, what of it? Who isn't sad in the evening?
How hard is it when candy is all that is coming?

Where is my deep green, where the trees for my bones?
Where the vines? Now may I have a vegetable?

In the olden days we drank fermented honey—a cup full
of blossom to be swallowed as often as possible.

Four then five asked if I was having a baby but I already had
and she was, as I said, pretty.

Pretty as her little sister and older brother. My husband
gave me a son to share with his mother, a little.

Remember billowing flesh back then? How like a red pear
I was, both sweet and fat.

How soft that new body tucked into pants. A fourth is not
forthcoming. No more cracking open in that way this body.

If the holiday foil-wrapped chocolates get any bigger I'll climb in,
take my milk blanket on the chin.

Not the same as rainbow chard with scarlet ribs and white string
to keep our respective teeth in their sockets,

nor a pocket full of spinach or handfuls of creeping thyme.
The children look like new potatoes, but louder.

The oil collects over dinner like fog with grease and we miss
those few weeks (dark green, damp and yellow)

in very early summer when you find whatever is even a little bit
ripe and ready to eat.

The Vital Function of Constant Narrative

Song of the Limpet

A lock says whatever is behind this door, you should not want it. The path beyond this padlocked gate, you cannot take it. Swimsuit dripping inside a locker, you can't have it.

The goggles mean the water will sting, that you can't see, question being, do you even belong here with the schools of fish?

Will you always end up shark-passed-over? Those goggles send tiny letters to both your eyes: Dear Whites, the salt will sting,

the nose bridge part will press your face, we are going to crease you a little. We think you should seriously consider a breathing tube.

Love from, two plastic cups with straps. Shoes tell you your feet are too soft, that you might need to skip someplace, but your two

little tenders won't want to take you that way, will leave like the key leaves the lock. It's only in for a minute, a visit of little twist.

Your feet will falter, send you sharp-worded telegrams about rocks and cuttlefish. Foot bones are so strangely brittle, a clumsy fall

cracks their stems like clams. Oyster shells cut your outer softness: feet into sea-ribbon, your envied fingers to strips.

Even your wrists are small-scale collars, easily turned crooked, little bits of meat feeling sore, discussing their tenderness.

The knuckles maturing like buds under water, swollen, moving, hinting
slightly, at something blooming, the redbud lung,

or lack of shell. What is dragging itself through the tide? A fossil fish
who's half in water. Leaning in on two liver-spotted fins,
she is grinding primitive shoulders.

The Vital Function of Constant Narrative

The Stuck Clock

In the living room it is always eight o'clock. No matter where I sit.
No matter how many glasses of wine.

No matter what I'm watching or who is talking, time never passes.
Four years of praying in this room—

God, send bits of cloth.
God, send red envelopes full of money.

Please let me die before my children but don't take me too soon.
Not tomorrow.
Not next Wednesday.
That's piano practice. Plus, I need to teach them
to think well of themselves, to save more than their mother did.

I have not taught them to bake bread.
What will they butter without me?

Dry ingredients first, then wet in the middle, like a lake.
Two or three eggs make the dough rich, almost like cake.

Sugar is food for the yeast; white flour or whole wheat
decides softness. Can they forage for dinner?

For children bread and water is not enough. Sonoma is on fire.
Here it is, acres later, eight o'clock and still no dinner.

Will you please give me someone who.
Something that.

No matter how strong the wind, the clock will not strike nine.
Ten doesn't come. Everything I shouldn't have muttered.

Suck back the hot words and curses from under my breath.
Anyone who talks like that does not deserve.

I am sorry for what I said. Dishes I threw. This is not a list. It is.
Before I ask for anything else, I should apologize.

Am I a girl, still? Hidden in the folds of my mother's dress?
Here it comes for your vineyards.

Here it comes for your red bottles. Here it comes for family.
Friends. Parking lots.

When the earth shifts and eats our brick buildings. Wood frames
floating like boats over soil. And still.

Look at the time. Hustle the children to brush their teeth
tuck them in bed with blankets like bread.

All of this I thought would push time through some pocket
but downstairs it's still eight o'clock.

The Vital Function of Constant Narrative

Black Mission Fig

Bore no fruit for the son of God who cursed one—immediately or within a few days it withered, died. If only the sun stayed longer overhead over winter I'd have dropped

my first fruit into that perfect hand. Where was the blessing for my branches and roots? Our rabbi spoke of a day-long battle allowing the Israelites to conquer giants—

old warriors living in the mountains bringing their flocks and bodies on horseback to plunder what they could; a sound like thunder or water pouring into the valleys and plains;

five of their fierce kings slaughtered when the sun would not set that day. If I had known, I would happily have given, but my leaves had only just begun to fan from branch buds. Too early,

too soon my finest minute ended in disgrace. You think I have nothing for you and you're right. I wish you'd waited in the shade for what I wanted to give, but you were in a hurry.

I had nothing bright or lustrous; for that I apologize, though it seems ludicrous, false to be sorry about the season or soil in which one is born. Fig flower nearly invisible and who isn't

in a certain light? If you can keep the sun stuck where it is mid-morning, hidden behind the cedar trees bordering the neighbor's garden, you can keep my children small so I can get this right.

Falling in love it's better to be less grateful and more precise. Nice is another word for flattened at the hands of another. We became a mutual hell, could not untangle our roots without killing parts

of each other—and we did. The fruit seed drops unplanned. To bloom again is a bargain with the land. It was years before I kissed another— even then I didn't get it right.

All my black seeds scattered or eaten, impossible to stop. Over and over I live that moment, missing the outstretched hand and the curse, then the heat, a thunder of hooves and thirst.

The Vital Function of Constant Narrative

BANG

Our universe began with the end of another. Now it's after dinner,
I'm standing at the kitchen window behind short, white curtains,
hand in a hot sink full of platters, hand hovering over cosmic dust,

though that is using the term loosely and includes the rough bark
of the loblolly pine and the swollen base of the water tupelo tree;
essentially everything.

The best thing about being grown up is grown ups can do whatever
they please unless they bow down to fear, loathing and bad habits,
the fate of most people I know,

thus their bad backs and wheezing, hearing loss, parking
tickets, chipped pots. I can't remember the last time
green unfurled to my fingertips and burst open like a halo overhead.

My chest was the devil's walking-stick. I kept my sorrow a secret
even from myself; no wonder I was giddy before the divorce.
I had no idea what was about to hit me,

which is how the universe works this time,
saddle-shaped or round; what's past the horizon you can't see until
it's about to go down: the baby heart whispering over its workload,

right chamber enlarged. Visible. Measurable. Baby ribs opening
down the midline making a bowl for the bypass machine.
Complex organisms prone to congenital, disastrous happenings;

praise the Western medical system that saved her. Had she died,
but enough of that, stardust. Cease compilation; divorce I handled
with two boxes of Ohio Blue Tip matches

and dead cassettes of the Rolling Stones. Praise the use of proper
names: Bristlecone. Colorado River. Aristotle. Jennifer. Tom.
Allentown. Damascus. Nostradamus. Strepto-

coccus. Even now our Universe rapidly expanding; already half
gone what was yesterday the outskirts and beyond.
Talk to unification theorists, physicists and cosmologists who see

a mathematical god. What compels us to expand? Why bother?
That kind of question tells you primary neurotransmitter levels
are down.

Serotonin reuptake inhibitors make a white gown for those of us
so inclined. Fred. Jean Hartshorn. Smelling salts. A bass player
for some unknown rock band who showed up coked up in Venice

and mostly wanted more cocaine. After the landslide in central
China, the wind caught in my chest,
it was either human dust or human experience: fear, grief, physics.

Thank God for praying on the late night sofa,
for *ask and ye shall receive.* Amen for even a little reprieve
and the bleach-scented hospital. Jupiter's red spot, its hurricane,

is back and I thank God for modern anesthesia, algebra, calculus,
and particle physics, the only body of knowledge in any of this
you can really believe.

The Vital Function of Constant Narrative

Ever After

I took a palmful of wine from a skull's silver dipper, licked
my hand dry, next in line, next in line, now a white scarf,

wrapped around the bride and groom, it's all new to them
and my chest is a breakable twig. That's why I cry so easily.

I am knit together with bows and pins, that's how marriage
seems to work: a few pricks, a furbelow, the dinner at home,
chores and so on. I leave off the mannerisms, one by one,

of the pretty girl. Instead of champagne, I get a bone scan,
most of my sticks a sturdy confection of rock candy,

both breasts perfect dumplings. This body ticking along
and for that we're glad, nothing breaks with a sneeze.

I'm ready to head home—find my husband in the car
then lose him twice on laundry day.
Laughing and yelling in equal fits.

What to do with happiness? Fold it into squares before any-
one can see, slip it under the bed like money or dirty books.

Call it a pig, feed it refuse by the garden. This is why they
teach us all about diamonds. A hard stone of great value

has nothing to do with becoming soft. That way you don't
look at your finger and weep; weep with abandon in traffic,
in the little grocery store where coconut milk comes cheap

in a can. Even when we're withered, walking with the help
of wheels or canes, we can tell ourselves *this time love stayed.*

Remember that much when everything starts falling apart—
the half-skull full of cognac, as if the brain distilled itself
for the quick pleasure of the heart.

The Vital Function of Constant Narrative

I Eat What the Goat Eats

Take both hands, lift up; bouillon and consommé cup.
Take hooves. If we trippingly go
where the politics

what?

Carrots, celery, leek; mirepoix and stickyweed cut up.
I eat what the sika eats but not from your pocket.
Not this time.

When I make coffee in the sink I let my second husband
drink from my cupped hands
locked together.

Last night I was sitting on the kitchen's rag rug
counting my blessings,
only kidding—lying down,

crying for the old days when everything I did
doubled in size—life was bread,
breath was butter,

two plump raisins for eyes. I eat what the deer
eat—wet grass and bark. No one does
your chewing for you, and that's fine.

In the bed, horizontal, no one else can do your sleeping
for you. And no one has a husband
as perfect as mine.

Second and Grand

Because of the rains two years ago, rain making weeds, weeds making seeds that fed mice and other rodents; snakes grew fat last year. The children admonished walked in hops.

Flying along the freeway puts us in peril but push the thought back and merge with traffic. Pretender to affection let pass.

When the smog rises up north it looks like art or tradition. People in cities see what they do wrong. Guilt strains the tendons and guy wires, shivers the one building covered in chrome that gets it right

when the sun comes crashing over the library. If there is a pot for every lid, introduce us. Four years makes all the difference when you graduated last in your class in high school.

All the heartbreak is ahead of us but luckily there is some behind. The sister who didn't die. The father who lives outside, the baby for whom we threw flowers into the river—

the mother who cannot process two people talking at the same time. Boom. Boom. Down for the count. I want to be thrown in the water too.

When you wait for something the event horizon stops your watch altogether. O the waiting. The balance shown by the deposit book is not to be taken as accurate unless verified by comparison with the bank's

The Vital Function of Constant Narrative

books. All orders for payment of money or salt; when in Rome, one does
and so on and so forth to the marriage bed. At first it seemed I would
never mind.

On second thought—
Where would you rather be? Standing in the half-
pace or slowly dying? Why not wait in a black box? See what comes?

Now he's off in the arms of upstate New York or walking his dogs.
A cousin in surgery. His mother playing guitar. Buying another house.

Those are three different people I will point out, none of whom know
my children, but the doctor I love with every rib and fiber. The day is

dying, sun finally setting over the yard where three snakes died.
Two women sit inside with three children and a white cake.

Everyone who knows you will parsiflake; speak a new language. Fossifi-
cate: become like bone, protect and harden. Pretty image,
that one. At night be what you are in daylight and then some.

Marlys West

The Knack of Dowsing

A gray geranium came in the mail with instructions to put
the flat stem in water. It should sprout a set of roots,
but the leaves were cigarette paper, the stem
had no good mouth

to take up the wetness. I didn't put the bloom in water,
did not snip the stem of that cracked flower, my faith
a farm dog running away, white hen in his mouth,
his days numbered, hers gone.

The post delivered reams of flatness, pressed love letters
and missings-you into hammered tin, into stacks of bills;
gas and oil going up, water leaking and people charged,
the leak a secret.

Someone sent a forked stick, a rod to find the underground
water. Cattle watched with fringed eyes; feed corn
on withered stalks ripened into rocks.

The mail was late, it was unwanted, whistling in a hinged
box, the paper wilting. In a pen a white sow leaned
alongside her litter. If anyone

approached the yard, she thrashed her legs, threw herself
against wooden slats, coarse skin coming through cracks
in ribbons. Piglets trailed her blue teats like comet dust,
streaks of ink.

The Vital Function of Constant Narrative

The letter paper was once wood, a folded envelope straining
to seal its orchards. Sour cherry trees picked over by robins
stumbled up the pasture hill near the gnarled apples.

The chewed-up hutch inhabited by dun-eared rabbits who
kicked their straw into dry, bitter piles. Barn mice
evaporated into thin air at the slightest sound

or unsettling of dust. In the henhouse I pulled my sleeves over
my wrists before reaching underneath
those bodies and taking eggs.

Marlys West

A History of Tranquilizers

I am busy today being a terrible hack: *her skin was white as snow*,
and all of that. Tomorrow I'll be simply charming, a regular darling,
the two-horse at the gate.

With my ankles wrapped, I'm usually blue, every race I throw a shoe
but people say I'm lucky.

My name is *Unfortunate Hapsburg Jaw*. Read my stall.
I come from *Champagne Filly* and *Raskolnikov's Purse*,
a regular blood letter so they feed me silver water, consult Ayurveda,

stick me with a pattern of aluminum pins and crack my back like a nut.
Ladies in hats waiting for tea, they're nothing to me, and to say fairly,

I'm little to them; the breath before watercress and mayonnaise,
a quick pause before liquor and losing another leather purse.
I've been interested in pantsuits since I was twenty-four.

Yesterday I saw what looked like a white rat; actually a napkin
in a shopping cart. Wind blew that paper back and forth.

It was locked in a cage desperate to get out. A brown woven blanket
across my lap made a man's head in repose, bereft and I wept
for his sadness or would have but something was off

and the image of his face dissolved until all I saw was the tail end
of some dark lizard. Unmoving.

The Vital Function of Constant Narrative

And then by my stable a white-winged bird, actually a second napkin.
Another imaginary animal from the paper mill. Nothing
captive after all, no disaster.

I'm skittish in the afternoon because the day takes ages to get through.
All I want is for the night to come and lay me down.

In the morning I'm prone to bolting, the horse that breaks your neck.
They haven't shot me yet. Girl swans in the chorus nod
their feathered heads in unison as the prince leaps across the stage.

His legs are knives and well they know it. He'll drop my sweet carcass
into water believing in some form I am his mother or father—
so not as besotted as I thought. What was that swirly drug
in the brown bottle?

It made my head feel funny, made my legs fall crooked on the dance
floor. I was late for the races, acting silly, talking and talking,

planning to write my memoirs, but wasn't sure who to write about;
an endless list of sorrows seemed dull, there was nothing else I wanted
to tell. I felt like hell; looked perfectly fine.

My picture got in the paper for the first time; someone poured champagne on my bridle because of it: *quid agis, agis bene:
what you do, do well,*

which was all I ever wished for, God help me. Think
back to when you were a girl, they said. Nervously, reluctantly, I did.

Marlys West

The Oddest Sea

Sing, Muse, in the old whimwham before terza rima. Holler
thy wine-dark dithyramb, Rose-Fingered Dawn, and so on;
how goes it? Whence and then some

until the actor shouted to an unseen stagehand: *drop the curtain,
man, bring up the lights.* All right, all right. Flagrant Delicto
followed by Scene-Cut-Shorto. Caught in the act, as I said.

Depicto, Restricto, Act One El Strippo as a matter of fact.

Underwear nubbins intact, knit sweater of red, brown and blue,
intimate halloo from land of white panties, land granting favors,
a savory pie you can add to the list of things to serve when

I die. Not for ages yet, keep your eyes wet without o'erspilling;
no swilling the wine of old emotions. Seven oceans keep us
apart, the whole love-you-till-death-do-us-part, that vow,

the honor and obey show, very dog and pony you know—sure
he's the one? At night is it singing you're full of
or sighing? Fake frying in the stage kitchen; faux egg scramble.

Nothing by halves, said the director. *Olde Marseilles
in the diaphragm. Project, project!*
Sorry Ma'am, no gas allowed onstage, therefore naught aflame.

The Vital Function of Constant Narrative

Thus pretend heat, same with the greasy salve when he burns
his back and acts as if his skin were tender. Fourth wall,
etcetera. Blame melodrama, his acclaim,

the actor's good-looking, bald-headed, buttock-y fame. Sing,
Muse, of the thread unraveled, of a wine-dark man who held
a burst chest.

His last look on life his best; dying as a play began, choking over
new love trickling up, chorus forced into ten-minute
remission.

To err, to die, is human, albeit flagrant delicto. Exit stage left
with small percentage of audience dead
and the first act nearly over.

Marlys West

Forsooth,

Someone keeps snipping our frayed bottoms off
and sticking our necks
in cold water. Tonight, nothing revives us.

Everything is *Hamlet*, *Othello*, and *Macbeth*.
I am sick to death of their lot.
Oh tragedy, oh fringy queen, that old scene.

What do they do with the stars at night?
Pluck them out as like as not.
What about the hired help?

Much help he turned out to be. *Tell me about it*,
he says. *Why do you think you feel this way?*
If this keeps up,

I'll never be cast in tragedy. Lady's maid again?
And how does that go? *Exit stage right?*
Bit part as Dunsinane tree? Lovely,

but I want back in the banquet scene,
chopping vittles for the Queen.
I neatly cut her vegetables up, a flick of the wrist

and the audience is mad for me. Peas and carrots,
indeed. I made up several lines of dialogue
and sapped the madness from the Queen.

The Vital Function of Constant Narrative

Tonight her dress is full of pins, such wonderful
sins we're enacting, I hardly call it acting at all.
Sit tall, milady, keep the pricks out.

I breathe in and out, like the rest of them. I am being
and not being this evening, speaking
sincerely and also deceiving.

Marlys West

Everything Twice

I saw you in front of the mirror elevating your arms, making four
limbs, a god of sorts, but no salt until salt is requested, as they say.
They meaning waiters. Same with water. To be sure, arrive early.

Well, husband, let's agree we are no longer young. Out of infancy
into paying a lender's fee. Here I am in this office building, white
and cream, listening.

The most beautiful tongue is Spanish and after that I love numbers
in English. One. Two. Three.
American English takes me ages to travel to the end of a sentence.

When you opened the front door to come in and your face flashed
with joy or unhappiness I could not tell if you were still in love.
Dinner was dull. You had a meeting with HR. Here we are.

If everything is created twice, first in the mirror then in the flesh,
there are many of you in the house. Here you are in each room
shining from every surface like a real husband.

I stood in my clothes closet without light next to the scarves; belts
behind me waiting for you to defuse yourself
but you never did that morning.

All day I waited for the fire to take your bones and break them
the way we break people when we bring them back
to life, each chest compression

The Vital Function of Constant Narrative

making a crack in the sternum which can only take so much. One,
two, three. The most beautiful tongue is French when Sophie tells
Charlie it is time for bed. The most beautiful post on the Internet

is when the boys on their bicycles write each other in Italian. *Caro
amico. Caro ragazzo.*
The most beautiful sentence lives in Vietnamese and its percussion.

If everything is created twice, first in the mouth and then in space
with dust and black matter slipping into every bed and body,
then here we are full of complications. Let us vote;

let us watch teeth like rain falling from the lips of the very
young, little beads.
Yes and no

their first words, then baby words for mother and father:
mama und papa
anyu és apu

making four, six, or eight parents, the mother in the morning,
the wife in the afternoon; language like a necklace hanging
just above the heart

as if the bones on either side and just below the darker hollow
in the throat
spoke.

.

Marlys West

If the River Sounds

It is carrying water. Meanwhile the children raise
their pitchy voices in displeasure.
When the mum screams she is harried; the father?
Has yet to come home.
This is how we disband: dinner all ready
and no one cares; when the mother grinds her teeth
in anger she is a witch.
      Cooking covers making potions,
absinthe and trousers,
wormwood powdered
out of French ghosts
wearing white-dusted wigs full of ostrich feathers
and tiny ships, satin dresses over silky underslips
and kid leather gloves. That's my breast, decorated,
      pale right hand
      holding a torch
to make the ocean sparkle. To make new gulls.

Sing to those ghostly white birds and homes the way
you speak to those you love.
One hand raised in anger
      is enough. The creek
behind our woods was dead
as I have mentioned.
Our forest was like no other; jack in the pulpit risen
brightly in the thick, green air:
bog onion, brown dragon,

The Vital Function of Constant Narrative

Indian turnip, wake robin, oxalic acid
ripe for sickness or death, we never picked it; strict
as Russian Orthodox bishops about it.
      In Moscow so it is in marriage:
long nights in a cupboard, onion domes at dinner,
another hour of perfectly useless talk
knitting us together. I'd have stuck it out but
that was not offered.
      My father advised me like a prince: no abject
begging or weeping in the tea but I laid no embargo
      on my own behavior.
To a mad dog ten miles is no great distance, they say
from the hut of some long and lonely winter.
Luckily I had the baby, her pink face a scalloped
shell, her big sister plump as migrating salmon.
      When the witch flies out of a pretty girl
      that is where I am going;
      from youth to evil,
      sugar cube tight between my two front teeth.

The first gift of tea looked like a load of dead leaves.
Who so brave
and drank it?
Remember the art of starting again; we do it every day.
      My name is never-
      forgetting water.
      Impossible. Plus
last year we couldn't reach the Chesapeake Bay, a long,
      wide tail of stones
and white spray;
even in the tributary river our motorboat felt too small

as the water grew choppy.
Now I know the sting of the tiny circumference
      that is my body.
Now I need to be liked again, no thanks to anyone.
It's been a long night over the books,
the girls asleep in bed, talking in squeaks and pips.

Do not say I am made of straw. A good mother
is the only easy path to happiness.
When I was very flimsy and despair swept up my bones,
but that is all in here.
      If I were out on the river again,
      I would love an aluminum hull,
         though it is too small. Love the engine, stalled,
      for the hope it gives,
love the fleeting company of winged fish, the sweet smell
      of salt water or black
      oxen in their pasture.
Love the ever-scowling neighbor who would help us now,
love her sullen, sideways children
and give them sugar. Keep it in your pocket
      and hand it out
      with songs of praise so that when
you speak of God on Earth, they remember.

The Vital Function of Constant Narrative

A Collision of Satellites

There is always debris, but how to make meaning of what we don't know happened? *Look for directions.* Look for an image of what didn't occur. Cook something up though the recipe is printed in a horsehair book the size of a fly and the print is faded green. Take three peppers, it reads. Or gippers. You're on your own if you can't read it and I know you can't read.

When I see art that doesn't make my head hurt, it's not real. When I read something that makes no sense, I know the writer is onto something. *Something!* I never make meaning if I can help it because someday all that meaning will be boxed up and rotten. I will be dead and finally you will know better, just like I know better and will never make any mistakes ever again, though good things came of it like our children and Barcelona.

Closer to home there's apiculture. The husbandry of bees. If you ask me, it's their business what they do in their hot colonies. Once upon a time there were directions for understanding etched in the black veins of each bee's white wing. Hold your bee gently by the abdomen and lift the wing-joint in order to read. *Welcome to the stratosphere.* This morning I knotted and knotted my hair. Here I am sitting in a friend's empty house eating her chocolate. Bits of foil satellite skin? Run for cover.

The lemon tree outside my window smells delicious and looks like its leaves are suffering some kind of black death. *There's your meaning.* Remember the natural world for reinforcement: note the little warbler's black cap, the slow swimming and monotonous curl of the horsehair worm in my backyard's plastic wading pool. Disgusting, but you've come this far.

They make meaning at the blacking factory, but then it's blacked out.
Dampered. So at one point we all knew, but for you it's still invisible
or a very dark blue like a late-night beach with green waves

reaching up cold sand. You could reach down and take up the broken
satellite pieces, black and yellow, hot with the sting from our atmosphere,
in your hand.

The Vital Function of Constant Narrative

Still Life Quail Leg on White Plate

Dark and sticky the sauce but the size of the ankle bone?
In the wild I could not catch this bird but here is a fey

bone like beach grass propped in the air. I'm on a date.
This was back when we first…

but he doesn't. I thought my heart would break open;
it didn't. In the front yard the Clementine tree is short

and gives off faint perfume; bees and babies love it.
You should know my children and I planted that tree

when it was a twig wrapped in a damp paper towel.
And now look

but you know this. You know my children are older
and I know your organs are slowly aging. Why

can't this bind us? My bones are in my body, pulling
at each other when I move myself: tilt the head,

arrange the slant
of my back so I sit up straight the way my mother said.

You can meet her someday. She is alive and healthy
and made of wax and petals. That is my mother flying

over you. My father is the ocean looking for sharks.
He will take their teeth out so surfers and swimmers

feel only the unpleasant sensation of being mouthed.
My sister and brothers are full of feathers. On our street

children run from one yard to another, all their faces
like windows smudged over, looking ahead

to what's for dinner
and if there is cake our mother is wonderful; how could

our father leave when she is made of wax and chocolate
and her bones are sticks of candy that never snap?

The Vital Function of Constant Narrative

Duck Egg as Low Poison

When they said *Head West!* I knew whom they meant and flew East
immediately, refused flights anywhere, never again, not for free

tickets or my own set of feathers. The forensics team asked
where I'd been hiding. They sent postcards full of egregious lies.

We all miss you!
We wish you!
Were here!

I asked the nurse to keep the mail in the hall so as not to suck up
the blasted oxygen. Bullocks to destination, the myth

of migration and four seasons, which run right into each other
as if they'd never heard of holiday or equinox.

How is that for fertility? You can head for the hills with your big
belly as long as you return for the baby shower
looking *luminescent.*

Such a good word, isn't it? A regular triple-hitter, a veritable *Versace*
gown, darling, don't forget it. To hell with reproduction.

Look what it did to the ducks, my friend. Back away
slowly from the brackish egg. Eat nothing
from the marsh.

Note the deer in the free world, the ticks and sickness they pass
on to us. Pathologists wanted to peel back the hair
on my skull, but I said to them wait one minute.

This is for what? It's a set up isn't it?

Forget about the living for a minute, the dead mad for celebration,
begging for marigolds and skulls made of sugar.

I come from the backwaters, land of crumbling
footwear, parish of brassy shades of hair, blue heron plucking
in and out of brackish water like a yellow wrist, algae a sleeve,

waving. Speaking of the old halloo, the woman who takes my blood
says scar tissue is ruining the only good vein I've got.

Needles plunge steel bills below the surface of my skin as if
I were a pond and the nurse a clutch of white ducks. *Sigh.*

If only she would pick me up, if only she might grease my wings,
if only when the pilot flies, he lets the autopilot sing.

The Vital Function of Constant Narrative

A Brief Collection of Villainous Faults

How pretty you look, reading this; the line of your jaw,
your lashes like black fringe on a living room curtain.
I know what you're thinking.

What's that sound in the midst of this? The chirrup?
It's a cricket in the broom corner of the kitchen.
At night he plays two notes: high then higher.

At first I thought it was a machine squeak. Washer?
Dryer? Refrigerator? Making ice?

Now you see I've come up in the world—wilderness
runs from my doorstep into a ravine. Root cellars
fade and the pump house stumbles to the ground.

Still, I wash everything every day. This is lower middle
class with child and I grind it; a finger pointing at truth
is not the truth, per se.

You heard the cricket, a symbol of good luck. *Chirrup.*

I can't believe how loud he is; can't believe what plain
language I'm using, as if a metaphor would hurt you
or shut the cricket up, stop the twang of his hind legs
or wings, whatever, banging. Crickets are a kind
of burglar alarm.

Once accustomed to the members of the household
they continue to chirp, stopping when a stranger
enters the room.

How grave you look, reading this, moon in your teeth,
twigs at your neck. This morning in every paper;
another dictator in the cellar of a farmhouse.

Evil faded just a little sitting in an old potato hole
listening to birds and wind, footsteps upstairs

putting his heart on a platter, on somebody's wedding
china—the faded leaves,
unidentified pink flowers.

The Vital Function of Constant Narrative

You Won't Be Needing This

The recipe said take two pigeons. From where? The roof?
I was stuck, too. Married five years then we were through.
How do you call birds for dinner?

Wear rings? Shiver seeds in the palm like sand?
Something refulgent is radiant, shiny, brilliant.
O tenebrous meal.

Why use words like that? I'll forget what they meant
when I come back with those two, blue ratty birds.

Lousy, lousy; insalubrious. Soporific:
to induce sleep. Hubris: overbearing pride on the part

of our family. It's bad when they won't let you waste
anything because *that would be wasting.*

Hungry, mad, I hid in the garden. Inimical: *dangerous.*
Dubious! Dark!
About the oleander in the front yard we said *go ahead,*

eat the poison leaves. The baby spoke to crows who knew
what she'd like and brought it. Crinkled things. Metal
spoons. How to keep the lambs happy?

Three walls, a vista plus daily hot mash. The rabbit hutch
was a flurry of suspicious activity. A ring of pellets
around their cage, black and shining.

A hundred greasy clouds make a herd of sheep, Wyoming
is where I was born last week. Not kidding.

When we moved to Los Angeles people asked what we'd do
when a big one came. *Call for help? Turn off the gas?*

Get under the table with the living things, hooves and claws,
wait for it to pass.

Cowed

When I was girl living in two worlds, the natural and the fabricated,
I found it hard to swallow.
Now there are specialists for that.

Out in the woods I was too busy to care if the lump in my throat
was a precursor to tears or the survival reflex shutting down
sections of the body it didn't need.

Below the tulip poplars I found a jack-in-the-pulpit, bright
and running with light poison.

I knew dark stripes could close a windpipe, same for any animal,
which I was. We gave that silk sock of the forest a wide berth
and felt it watching from its perch

on the hill. More beloved was the skunk cabbage, broad leaves
on either side of the creek giving off their spicy,
foul smell,

the basis of most of our toxic concoctions as was the pokeberry
dripping purple-black fruit, entire plant a cholinergic poison.

Beneficial to humans the silver-barked sassafras whose saplings
we pulled up to chew. It made your spit smell good.

Impossible to climb trees circled with shining poison ivy,
leaves mottled red, black and green, it would cover our limbs
with a mess of tiny bubbles
by nightfall—instead I found a perch in a sugar maple past

our backyard's back gate, no one could see me. I read books
in that tree like an airborne speckled rabbit,
young and jittery,

I hopped down and ran around. As a new mother everything
wore me out with worry.
If I heard two little hiccups I jumped. *Is she choking?*

Her father hoped I was joking but even now I'm not kidding.
As a girl I saw cats where cats were not
and dogs where stood nothing—
mind you, this was all indoors: socks, bikes, handbags
full of yarn, lamps. Even now I look with suspicion
on anything relatively normal

because on second glance it never lasts. What was it
the other day? Some animal flickered past

but I didn't pay attention because I know how creatures
move when they are real: the dart and slink, skitter
and leap.

Twenty years ago one summer cabin camping, a black snake
fell into my arms when I let down the window's
eyelid shutter. To this day no one in the family believes that.

The Vital Function of Constant Narrative

But I tell you, *you who are so dear to me*,
it's true, I felt that weight like a prosthetic leg

and the thump when I dumped the roiling creature to the peeling
porch sticks with me to this day.

Marlys West

Marry the Donkey

Braying all night, trampling straw, I was an animal
made for work. Beneath the evergreen trees, long

pine needles made the ground springy and the wind
made clouds of fine yellow powder. It was spring-

time when the first wave of dissatisfaction, smoke-
like in the distance, made me look up from grazing.

Sitting in her black chair the counselor said, plough
forward; said to hold ourselves deeply accountable,

whatever that means. When one of us cried my mind
wandered. That's fiction. A lie. Something written

at the cost of what happened. As indicated there was
a counselor, gray hair and boots looking at the roots

of our problem weekly; it's not cheap to be unhappy.
I think it started with his fallen arches. That's fiction,

too. Both of his feet are fine. This isn't a confession.
I'm talking about the essence of marriage the way one

might discuss a dark sky over two heads unprotected.
Feathers fell from the open breast of a dove. That's

The Vital Function of Constant Narrative

your background. I cried through our marriage vows,
a little damaged, not pathetic, wedding cake cunningly

decorated with fake ants; not fiction. I asked for ants
to go with the summer picnic theme; the cake came

with a black sugar string of them looking like stitches,
which seems now (heads up: more fiction) prophetic.

Marlys West

Flowers Keep their Original Yellow

Sickness evaporates like water, the lake is blue paint and glitter.
No one leaves in the arms of fleeing militia.
Dark spots refuse to map out lungs.

Every sunset the office buildings turn to gold, the secretaries
who work there hold their breath in happiness,
chip at the walls in between answering calls,

accumulating massive fortunes. On the left sit clay mountains;
blue-purple. When a train comes, you hear the engine sing
through the worm-glad earth

and the station bursts into color. Commuters arrive stacked like
crackers, envelopes pressed together that fly over the elevated
platform, delicate as silver leaf,

not quite bursting into a third dimension. A woman as a ribbon
cannot taste what is going to happen.
There are stitches in between her breasts.

Her old life is candle smoke and all her clothes in a faraway
closet are nothing but white wax stuck together.
Sleeves go wrong like that; a finger can't get through.

The man behind her gives her his last rib and a ring, too.
She says, *I think this means we're married. Yes,* he says,
we're a family; if we have a baby, she'll be a pressed flower.

The Vital Function of Constant Narrative

Afterwards, they lay in bed like paper fans unfolding, chests full
of tin. Bones like emotion. Their house made of plastic
if you have to ask, but don't.

In the gold there is a room upstairs where the woman's hair falls
thick and fine. Her trees are moss on sticks
and the grass is glued-down sand.

She wears her hair pulled back, her lungs like saffron blossoms.
The infant sleeps in a wooden crib, a black-haired letter
from someplace divine.

Marlys West

The Vital Function of Constant Narrative

If the world is but a place of language, at last I know wherefore I talk too much.
To make a place for myself, to create out of every ten sentences a bed to lie in,

a chair for sitting; and of the next ten sentences, even little glitches like glitches
like like,
for example, strong proof the machine is not running down to dead. Sputtering
to life, a stuttering, thus I speak in the rambling monologues reserved for small
children who know their mother is not paying attention and must walk through

her tiny ruffle of neglect, that familiar shiver of invisibility. The child talks loud
and long about nothing; merely the act of throat humming, the fact of air passing

over vocal chords that makes the difference.
It is the opposite of quiet which equals dead,
always hard to live with. Mom, watch me wink, Mom, can you shut one eye?

Mothers go on faith that their children are human. We have no choice, though a baby is incomprehensible. Just so, I believe the white gorilla

The Vital Function of Constant Narrative

would not be understood by anyone other than her trainer busy inter-
preting every
blink and finger twitch into actual communication. Coco want a kitty?
Coco want
lunch? I tell you we all do it, make meaning when meaning isn't there—
the ape

probably dreaming of the jungle, the children asking for some little proof
of existence, the mother dreaming of something equally rare, her
crammed-up

thought processes thick as smoke and the children talking as if they
know that now,
now, now their mother will pay attention though she has no choice,
really
just a slight inclination to do so.

Marlys West

We Made You Out of Wax

so that you would live forever and ever, bar a hot
day, or too-warm water, or someone holding you

for an hour. You are the first offspring, an offering
to the world, our candelabra, the magic we made,

the abracadabra and there you were, dove-rabbit,
too small to be seen, but the heart beating, tucked

like a mite in a soft pillow, a brown weevil in five
pounds of flour. Later we watched you kick at my

ribs. Much later it was you crying in the hallway
because our old dog wouldn't get up and come to

you the way she usually did. She won't get up for
anyone, not until she's ready, so she must not be

ready. We sent you back to bed with that logic,
down the long hallway to your very own room

where the dog was sighing and your body seemed,
at night, to be something we made up on a whim,

something that we might unravel or unbend, but
not unkindly, perhaps as we slept or watched color

The Vital Function of Constant Narrative

television. It might happen blindly in the grocery
store, a rifling through beet greens as you dwindle,

flesh to candle, from that to the wax they dip each
eggplant into, to make the purple deepen in luster.

SMASH

At night every object in the bedroom looks gray: walls
and curtains, damp clothes hanging like Spanish moss.

Outside sodium vapor burns the air orange
and turns flying insects black as the shadows floating

underneath neighborhood cars. Up and down the block
children rest in rows after hours of shouting.

In bed their bodies look like silk socks and wigs. If only
the grass looked green out back and the weary could roll

like horses. But at night we do as the air bids—grass
a black and yellow carpet. When you are in love

the world is loud in your ears: *Hermosa, Beloved, Sweetie,
My Dear.* I hear a tick in the clock and the dog next door

muttering, crows chattering into their wing feathers
like distant traffic.

When the children stay with their father the house blooms
around me like a magic box. I am unmoored

without the usual ration of dishes, clothes and milk.
The clean house is a comet that cuts my throat
and makes a bowl of my bones.

The Vital Function of Constant Narrative

I take myself to church. It is Good Friday; a preacher
with long hair and a white shirt says love your neighbor.

Around us the room is dark and starry, my hand in the hand
of an old stranger who strokes it.

For ten minutes he is my milk and folding clothes, dishes
waiting for their daily bath, for the rushing hot water
and peppermint soap.

Marlys West

When the Coward Goes Out

I am eating the wing of a honeybee, my tepid life is a glass of tea.
Remember the sound of the gold trombones,

the flick of the carpet, glimmering red, meat served on alabaster
platters, dim light, dimly flattering the bastards.

They said I was great in my day, always nervous or chipper,
a glass slipper ready to shatter.

If the earth's tilt or my father's cigarette had shifted,
there's no telling who might sit here quaking.

The third revolution worked like a charm and broke the poor
stick of my back. The critics laughed up their sleeves at you.
They said, honey, you are through.

I was an anteater then, sleeping pills my ants. I washed them
down with milk, or was it water? No matter.
Death said, I hate my life.

In the middle of the night, the march of the infarctions starts,
followed by trumpets of tremors and strokes.
All night long I rush back and forth,
pushing the dead into paddleboats.

My wife's name is Grief. Her hands are bells with writing
on them. In God Our Lamb, and so on. Let us be cake.
Death requests you hold your clappers.

The Vital Function of Constant Narrative

Early bells, forged sheet iron, rang for celebration and signaling.
Enemy at the gate, for example, time for dinner.

They carved the roast in slivers fine as slipper soles. Potatoes
like stones, came a dozen for everyone. Sugared almonds,

smooth, white teeth full of secrets, smiled in their baskets.

Lastly the mushrooms, not all of them good; party in gastronomic
agony, I ran through the woods. Thought to hide with the choir
in a valley, but they kept to their singing, giving me away

immediately. *Oh, he sits amidst us!* Who will save the kingdom
from burning? To this day we don't know the composition
of a chemical substance called Greek Fire;

a mess wrapped in linen that burst into flames in water.
It contained sulfur, saltpeter, path, naphtha, charcoal,
possibly wax.

I crawled on; lived in a tree, more ape than man, more fruit
than beast. When the soldiers came for dinner,
I hid in the shed and would not come out.

Everyone said I was very pleasant and would do well
once I buckled down. Instead I knuckled under;
nodded my head as if I were dead but my neck still worked,

a bit of a hinge, mostly a fool. The critics said, you should
have seen yourself. You were funny as a set of lungs
gasping,

a kidney wincing at passing urine, which is to say, you made
us antsy, you hussy.

Milksop, Pantywaist, Foolish-Elastic; names are plastic
and last an age, past the empty plaza
of the mercantile exchange,

past water sitting in Windsor Castle's drains, a collection of strip
malls, wildly unhappy dogs
scratching the dry earth with black and yellow claws.

Death says shake my paw. Carry my scythe, why don't you?

Steal my beloved.

My poor wife, her name is Grief. She's a thief, all sticky fingers
and milky hair. My poor wife is a venerated saint. Her bells

are thin as the skin of birds, we divide her finger bone into thirds.
I sew her knuckles into my coat pocket,
and hold her sandal, like a lantern, aloft.

The Vital Function of Constant Narrative

A Study in Accidents and Disrepair

The tinsnips lost their fine edge to a stout wire slipped
between the blades, more of a stick or twig that wire,

not meant to be cut, but I pressed the handles together
and chipped the still blade's finish. Blue, blue, that half-

second after you've ruined something. This was just
whole, you say. So completely intact, whatever it was,

vase, bottle, jar of mayonnaise, now smashed. That's
my fault, too, rushing through the kitchen at lunchtime,

I took too many things from the icebox. Haste makes
a mess, they say; takes a piss, forgets. Glass-studded

globs of mayonnaise sat on the kitchen floor, stunning
but festive, too, the white sparkle and shine. Despite

washing the spot for an hour, the dog would not stop
licking the linoleum. The kitchen smelled of rot after

that, a smell of defeat, of mold, crevices impossible to
reach. No soap or brush will clean this, there is no god

to pray to; he's busy with wind or wars, and like the dog
told to knock it off, quit licking that spot, will not heed.

Marlys West

Encyclopedia of the Dead

It is rumored that dust is their handbook. The glow of light
in the night sky opposite where the fat sun sets, yellow

and faint, is the last few rats on fire in the kitchen
of the nighttime stars. It is said the dead live above the oven.

They are made of milk and pie, all sugar, their hair
pale and sticky. Some think the dead are candy.

In this world they're dust specks shining. They move beneath
doors of spilt milk, they are flat as dimes but evaporate

soon enough. We hear them in the late night breeze,
sleeves brushing air; they are scented with rosemary talcum

powder and drop tiny, blue flowers for cigarette ash over
rooftops and sky. The dead are not like you and I;

they've worn the last black coat and mittens. The dead
are limber, can touch their toes, mostly they pose limbs

akimbo, a circus of wonder contortionists without bones.
Weekends the dead live on their trapezes where they swing
as if the walls weren't there. The masses see nothing but

peanut shells because the dead never get the show started
on time. Who'd even have them for dinner? Dead is not

The Vital Function of Constant Narrative

as good as roast beef or coarse-cut black tea in a jar. Dead,
they see everything and swing right through it, legs fly up

like frenzied dancers. It sounds better than it is; they envy
everything. Late at night they sing sad tunes, filling the pantry

with sour notes, turning vermin green with longing; the dead
are toothless, worthless, sighing. They sift sorrow like baking

powder or soda. The dead fly through the kitchen crying,
making cakes fall; brown weevils lay their tiny eggs with
warm blessings to counteract that sorrow.

Unbecoming

Around the island the water's dark beauty is mostly unfathomable.
Same for the sky. Overhead the monarchs come thick as sparrows.

Here I am a deer like other deer.
Here I am a white-tailed rabbit.

Tick-bitten I slip through island woods for sweet grass and water.
White-winged moth stuttering over dunes and gorse berry knots—

I am also a moth of sorts—at times a little drunk, at times
ungainly.

For lunch I eat eggs the way a fox
might, afterwards stretch like a green snake behind the house

while striped bass loom black underwater. At night the bats and I
skitter over the porch.

Am I not a mouse with mouse concerns? The seeds, my seven soft
ones, this little nest in the attic?

Dead rabbit with your still-wet eye who will take you into the low
woods?

The Vital Function of Constant Narrative

Spun

Why did you tell me about the humpback whale? The male
singing through his nasal cavities, sounding for hours on end

and to what purpose? Love and territory? Delicious the fin-
sluice of water against his body? Why must I know white-

tiled Turkish baths where old men come to soak their heavy
limbs? It is not about male: the moon is dark with basalt,

for example; milk and blood cannot truly be duplicated.
It is all so beautiful it's emptied my head. Only wind in here.

Ocean basins became black plains. Also the sky and clouds
that even today deserves more than a glance, but I am only

under that broad, blue expanse for as long as it takes me to get
to my car. I am a woman sitting in that car. With children
in the backseat, one of whom can buckle herself in, the other

learning and furious to do so. And the car itself a rolling bed
of dust and crumbs, sand, sticky things, old gum and paper.

Now you understand why the bottles buried in the Baltic
Sea are dragging me down to their now-empty silt sockets.

I know nothing about those narrow-necked hollow caskets
except that I want to lie there forever and watch the fish

pass over. But I am on dry land dragging through long
days like a donkey, leftovers decomposing in a sink

full of dishes. I cried into the black onions. Once
I bought lemonade in a can, seven lemons

on the label and it turned out to be black, unsweetened
tea. So in addition to every natural wonder I can't fathom,

there is a beverage factory to think about, the sheer wonder
over the robot packaging and more delight over actual filling

of lemon-decorated cans. I don't want this wonder, I'm late
already. This I don't know: whether or not the moon spins.

How happy I am not knowing. How glad I am that it might
be a dumb round chunk of coal up there in the sky, a white

bowl, something hovering for all humankind, a ball of iron
with a silver face. It is a rock as I am a creature, an organism

with a certain life cycle. There is no reason for me to make
more of that dead circle than I just did—still I must do it

and wonder a little how it hovers, where it comes from, if
there is a smell to its dust and craters roasted under the sun.

The Vital Function of Constant Narrative

When the President is Black

some old-timey people will say, I always did like people of color. There was this one lady
who looked after my mother, O trusty soul, if I put a twenty dollar bill on the table, she'd
act like it was a hot coal. You couldn't tempt that woman to steal or do wrong. Seven gold
candlesticks my mother owned and eight she had when that nice lady left. They say African-
American now. Anyway, my mother was bereft, but it was time for her to go to a nursing home
to be properly looked after. From diaper change to the hereafter. The last time I saw my brother,
Chris, he had nothing to say about mother or any of this, he was busy with the Renaissance
fair, making costumes, getting his hair to grow in that weirdo bowl cut that passes for men
of yore. He wanted that sword from Toledo our long-dead father brought back, but I said
no, thinking it would get a good sum on block. That was the last time we spoke, even though
we're orphans. Doesn't that count for something? Apparently not. He found God. I asked him about the lamb in Revelations with seven horns and seven eyes, and if he thought that animal
was some modern, nuclear invention, but Chris never said a word because I was a heathen
to him by then, and his brethren wouldn't let him do anything but collect the check from

the auction and move on. Have fun with the new hair shirt, I called after them. You know
how cults work; it's all God, God, God, and, as an afterthought, your savings and wages
just to get the good word going around, not for anyone's benefit, you see, though anyone
can calculate it cost lots of money to smoke grass and lure a bunch of youngsters to some
dirty temple in the woods, but never mind, oh, never mind me, I'm the one who stayed behind
who didn't go off with the brown shirts. I said, show me a book where beasts have six wings
each, where one has the face of a man, and I'll happily show you a work of fiction, but they
said I hadn't got the proper spirit in me and wasn't worth converting. Pisser. One time my
brother, that's Chris, told our mother about the four horsemen: the white and red, the black
with his scales and malice, and the last horse, a pale horse. Apparently not white. She said
do you mean the President? God damn it all, I whispered to nobody. But here's the thing
I liked. The thing that made sense was the part where you shake a fig tree and she drops her
fruit because she has no choice, it's not about figs being ripe. It's that you asked and you got.

The Vital Function of Constant Narrative

He Must Have Hung Us Up to Dry

Two rows of bitter greens bound the winter garden. Hard peas sat underground,
wrinkled brains blinking under a sprinkling of soil,

round windows in a buried town. In an old stone coop, egg-laying hens curled
their rock-like yellow feet under warm feathers. Stars did not come out,
though the evening was ripe with heads under wings
like figs hidden in an old fig tree.

In the yard a pale green egg—a jade eye plucked from an idol left behind
in a midnight raid when devotees fled their stations.

Smudge sticks gave forth sweet smoke and died,
a telegram from the act of burning. A girl in the temple took excellent notes.

You might write, "Temple fell," she said. Stop. Thatch remained intact
and bells hung under the eaves like bats. *We must be flowers,* they said.
Our blooms ring when the wind blows.

Is anything else worth growing? We didn't know. Couldn't say.
The lettuce,
so low, had no idea. Shyly, she put forth fringy leaves. *I see I'm beautiful.*

The peas stuck it out underground. It was weeks before they uncurled,
it would feel like years. They knew life was once air and light,

dark was different. But why turn hard as rocks? Where was the old softness?
They astonished themselves. Nothing cracked them.

The idol was a one-armed farmer. They never caught him weeding, just sitting
as if he had nothing to do.

Ladies buttered his limbs each morning, believing he was a god of happiness.
They made a clay arm and wept over him. One night his face was taken apart
and the eye fell out of some thief's pocket.

A bantam chicken, small and dark, looked back as she walked the temple yard,
there sat the egg, still warm and living, waiting for a downy underbelly.

Her dirty legs made the perfect hollow,
that's what the idol saw: a great bird running at him, stick legs upon him then black.

The Vital Function of Constant Narrative

How Many Moths Make the Weight of the Moon?

Among the flatware insects clattered, their legs dumb
twigs bent back by knees. Weeks flew by with dishes

dirtied, conquered. We gave hurrahs, made anxious
toasts, *here, here*. The light brought flittering things.

In the morning on the porch the dead made a carpet
of dried bodies. In an animal world I blamed my

housekeeping and used two hands for your coffee.
You took the tepid, brown water from my cupped

fingers and sugar ants patterned the white kitchen.
One night you mentioned means of deterring vermin:

boric acid along the walls, chrysanthemum powder
sifted under the sink, disks made of poison. Food

stains grew soft flowers. I wonder how we held back
disaster? Two sips of water and a squeeze of lemon?

I don't remember. A fly landed in the butter; sticky
paper was zip to him, in the dark it always got us.

Bright as a torch I lit the house to keep us from sticking,
light calling the night beetle and moth; ants did not veer

from their anointed path over the linoleum. Nor did
you. It was time for bed when the crusts of toast bowed

down holding hems of sticky jam. Outside in answer
the moon sank under the weight of those soft carcasses.

The Vital Function of Constant Narrative

Signs of Imminent Breath

Just before she was born I said to everyone in the room, please
please, quit talking; I'm trying to be something other than love's

sticky weed. So often we get it wrong. Let's not get started on
reproduction. God knows I've studied since I was young and saw

a fat black rope dangling from a dusty horse. We girls wondered
how it was tied there and why. *O Lordy*, we said, understanding.

That's no rope! 'Twas the whole shebang so to speak; we screamed
in the back seat of the blue van and made our mother look the other

way so she wouldn't know we'd seen. Over there, we pointed.
What's in that barn? Near-disaster. Sex for the mare must mean

to disembowel. *Seppuku.* We were, to our great relief, still virgins.
Who wanted to grow up? It looked so grim and disgusting: stiff

gray hairs and weird spots. Old people thought we looked like
roses. *Live every day as if it's your last.* That made me nervous—

the worst suggestion I ever heard. I asked the doctor if I could
see the placenta. It took two hands to hold up. *That's no purse!*

Last winter I did nothing but knit peptides together. After I had her
my long hair came out in the shower. I could knit a second mother.

Soon enough my body flattened, bread of my morning turning to sugar
water for the baby under a bulb in a plastic box, the new daughter.

Marlys West

Ganzfeld Los Angeles

So dark it was the dogs would not walk, not one of them
and our eyes spinning in their sockets
like the eyes of someone in a cartoon

who had been hit, hard, and knocked over the side
of some steep cliff
first suspended for a second as if gravity were another

option to choose from
candy store-style, licorice in bins, sticks of black, green,

red, sticky jelly hearts and soft teeth
smelling like strawberry, tiny black tires

full of salt and hardness
spit out by the street until the sidewalk clicks when

you step on it. The room was magic even if it was a museum
made to look that way, colors soft and bright as blush,

lipstick and eyeshadow, cat collars, gems you stick all
over your face;

colors changing that white room
and annex every shade of pink, blue, orange, green and gray.

The room rounded like candy and powdery-looking
but every object in the room, meaning other people,

The Vital Function of Constant Narrative

perfect strangers, in sharp focus,
creases and eyelashes outlined and almost harsh

but the air diffuse and the doorway we climbed in
up the black steps also changing. All night our eyes felt

the light of other places; the sharp blue dots on bar glasses
the chandeliers and their glow, even the white plates
put forth a shine

as the black cod glistened in sauce; wine put a red shift
into the atmosphere
as if we were falling apart or flung distant from every
other object, just far enough to pull together

beneath a sign for dry cleaning and cars zipping past
eyes open wide and white to catch the light
please tell us where to go, they said, please make a path.

Marlys West

Regret and Other Bodies

The electrocardiogram showed one of the heart valves,
I don't know which one and this is the longest set up
for one tiny image

to the point where I have to question why I bring it up,
only let me be clear it's to point out my own loneliness
and face wet with tears,

which has nothing to do with the valve waving like a white
branch. Each heart contraction starts with a little tree
fluttering madly.

A cartoon of a twig waving hard over blood then nothing.
Perfect, said the doctor. How do I look at my daughter
when she wants to go home and play without me?

With a face full of love and distraction. Is it my phone ringing?
Everything I am now trying to play standard isn't working

but this is false, I already went over it with a dear friend
who says the time to question your life is never

seven days after someone looks at you and says he can't,
he just can't, it's all so tiring. It's so bad his hair is falling.

Meaning me.
Meaning him. Meaning I ignored the signs because

The Vital Function of Constant Narrative

truthfully we were through and I couldn't stand his topics
of conversation. I had better things to do.

I put my children in the care of the nanny who is young
and full of promise. That ship has sailed, we said.

There are some opportunities that never come again
but are we not inhaling the air as I write and you read?
Are we not alive and able to lift our heads even slightly?

Where is hope, that sharp fork that puts sugar on everything
like rain wets earth
telling every weed's seed and grass root to come up
because now all drought will be forgotten, never again
the long summers without someone watering and watering

but we know this isn't true. And yet we go on sprouting
and cutting our hair and wondering if this goes with that—
does it go?

If the countertops should be granite or poured cement
or if tile is what we should be thinking,
every new place in town

using longer white tiles for now but you know it will wash
up on the beach in ten years, chips smooth and rounded

like teeth; children picking them up and asking their mother
if they can keep the mouthful.

She says put them in your pocket and stop collecting every
shell. She says: there is sand in your hair and everywhere,

lunch is already full of grit and it took me over an hour
to pack up. Where is your father and don't spill all the water.

But when she stands up to dip her own body in the water every
harsh word is nearly forgotten because she is up, the mother,

heading for the breaking edge of the white water. A miracle,
her body, and how she doesn't care about the spit and spray,

cuts through all that pounding water with her arms and legs
she who brought us forth with equal parts love and shouting.

The Vital Function of Constant Narrative

Courage

Just now I swallowed half a pill and wished for the tenth time
that I was young again and pretty. Pretty kept me busy, Allen.

Engaged four times or so I like to think, but only once with a
ring. Now I have faded, Philip, but so have you, a little. Who

knew? Nobody ever thinks good looks are anything but their
own doing; I'm looking at you, Franco. The photo on the back

of my next book will be nonexistent or small. To Joseph, Mike,
Andy and Sean, the ginger-headed boy on the ferry to Dover.

It took ages to cross over, he and I. Benny, Dennis, Eddie,
Tom who swore I was an angel when he nearly died, high,

standing like a marble statue in the path of an electric train.
I held him back from the tracks, held him fast, as sheet metal

wrapped into loaf shape flew past. He took a look at my white
face and took off shouting he'd seen God. He'd been eating

hashish cake all day and looked like a beautiful buck gone
insane. When I find true love I'll have to look the other way,

walk my children home from a long day of shopping because
we're all of us too knotted up from the red grapes to witness

the revelation and are beginning to fray. Once my stroller
lost a wheel and I got my arm caught in the big girl's bike;

I could have collapsed under the mean-smelling gingko tree
with its yellow fan-shaped leaves scattered around me, only

I'd have had to get up eventually and brush everyone clean.
I remember my slender mother wearing Chanel Number Five

and a wide-legged white pantsuit looking so lovely even now
I could cry. Dear Eric and Sam: I'm better for being a mother.

Despite long hours and interminable chores, I am absolutely
more alive. Everything everywhere runneth over; I brought
children into this world and didn't even try. Better than cork-
necked squash in a garden and louder, hotter. At night I sleep

next to each child; their hearts beat faster than mine, like sleeping
with wind-up clocks. *Tick* and then in a rush the tock. I was glad

when the baby grew out of asthma long enough to hear the hole
in her heart. Glad in the sense that I almost screamed through

an office and cried that Friday in the middle of temple. Luckily,
Arthur, Tom and Noah, it was something modern surgery

could fix and so they fixed it, her ribs opened like a crown roast
then stapled back together into a lung cathedral. Weekdays

I keep an image of both girls, their wispy hair and long bones,
in my brain's aching pocket, wait a few minutes in the school

parking lot before starting up the dark windowed four-door white
car and heading off.

Acknowledgements

Kindest thanks to the editors of the following periodicals and anthologies in whose pages these poems first appeared:

American Literary Review: "He Must Have Hung Us Up to Dry"
American Poetry Review: "By that I do Mean Horse"
                                   "When the Coward Goes Out,"
Baltimore Review: "Regret and Other Bodies"
Boston Review: "When the President is Black"
Blackbird: "The Oddest Sea"
Cimarron Review: "The Spin of the Chores in a Secret Pocket"
Comstock Review: "Ever After"
The Cossack Review: "Who Came Before"
Crazyhorse: "Flowers Keep Their Original Yellow"
Duende: "Still Life with Quail Egg"
Hayden's Ferry Review: "Encyclopedia of the Dead"
Indiana Review: "A History of Tranquilizers"
Midwest Quarterly: "Song of the Limpet"
Notre Dame Review: "We Made You Out of Wax"
Paragraph: "Marry the Donkey" (originally "Tooth")
Ploughshares: "Forsooth,"
Quercus Review: "Signs of Imminent Breath"
Women's Studies: "Duck Egg as Low Poison"
                         "Knack of Dowsing"
Zyzzva: "A Study in Accidents and Disrepair"
Zocalo: "Vital Function of Constant Narrative."

www.ingramcontent.com/pod-product-compliance
Lightning Source LLC
Chambersburg PA
CBHW071252070526
44583CB00017B/2429